HAL•LEONARD
INSTRUMENTAL
PLAY-ALONG

TENOR SAX

GREAT MOVIE THEMES

CONTENTS

To access audio visit:
www.halleonard.com/mylibrary
Enter Code
2734-5047-6478-3418

Audio Arrangements by Peter Deneff

ISBN 978-1-4950-0556-5

HAL•LEONARD®
CORPORATION
7777 W. BLUEMOUND RD. P.O. BOX 13819 MILWAUKEE, WI 53213

Visit Hal Leonard Online at
www.halleonard.com

BATMAN THEME

TENOR SAX

Music by
NEAL HEFTI

GABRIEL'S OBOE
from the Motion Picture THE MISSION

TENOR SAX

Music by
ENNIO MORRICONE

THE GODFATHER
(Love Theme)
from the Paramount Picture THE GODFATHER

TENOR SAX

By NINO ROTA

LAST OF THE MOHICANS
(Main Theme)
from the Twentieth Century Fox Motion Picture THE LAST OF THE MOHICANS

TENOR SAX

By TREVOR JONES

GONNA FLY NOW
Theme from ROCKY

TENOR SAX

Words by CAROL CONNORS and AYN ROBBINS
Music by BILL CONTI

HE'S A PIRATE

from Walt Disney Pictures' PIRATES OF THE CARIBBEAN:
THE CURSE OF THE BLACK PEARL

TENOR SAX

Music by
KLAUS BADELT

MRS. DARCY
from PRIDE AND PREJUDICE

TENOR SAX

By DARIO MARIANELLI

MY HEART WILL GO ON
(Love Theme from 'TITANIC')
from the Paramount and Twentieth Century Fox Motion Picture TITANIC

TENOR SAX

Music by JAMES HORNER
Lyric by WILL JENNINGS

NOW WE ARE FREE

from the Dreamworks film GLADIATOR

TENOR SAX

Written by HANS ZIMMER,
LISA GERRARD and KLAUS BADELT

OVER THE RAINBOW

from THE WIZARD OF OZ

TENOR SAX

Music by HAROLD ARLEN
Lyric by E.Y. "Yip" HARBURG

THE PINK PANTHER

from THE PINK PANTHER

TENOR SAX

By HENRY MANCINI

STAR WARS
(Main Theme)
from STAR WARS, THE EMPIRE STRIKES BACK and RETURN OF THE JEDI

TENOR SAX

Music by
JOHN WILLIAMS